More of The World's Best Irish Jokes

In this series:

The World's Best Dirty Jokes
More of the World's Best Dirty Jokes
Still More of the World's Best Dirty Jokes
The World's Best Irish Jokes
More of the World's Best Irish Jokes
Still More of the World's Best Irish Jokes
The World's Best Jewish Jokes
More of the World's Best Jewish Jokes
The World's Best Doctor Jokes
More of the World's Best Doctor Jokes
The World's Best Dirty Stories
The World's Best Dirty Limericks
The World's Best Dirty Songs
The World's Best Aussie Jokes
The World's Best Catholic Jokes
The World's Best Mother-In-Law Jokes
The World's Best Russian Jokes
The World's Best Fishing Jokes
The World's Best Salesman Jokes
The World's Best Computer Jokes
The World's Best Scottish Jokes
The World's Best Cricket Jokes
The World's Best Golf Jokes
The World's Best Maggie Thatcher Jokes
The World's Best Lawyer's Jokes
The World's Best Business Jokes
The World's Best Holiday Jokes
The World's Best Acting Jokes
The World's Best Drinking Jokes
The World's Best Gardening Jokes
The World's Best Motoring Jokes

Des MacHale

More of The World's Best Irish Jokes

Illustrated by Louis Silvestro

ANGUS & ROBERTSON

An Imprint of HarperCollins*Publishers*

AN ANGUS & ROBERTSON BOOK

First published in the United Kingdom by
Angus & Robertson (UK) in 1984
An imprint of HarperCollins Publishers Ltd
First published in Australia by
Collins/Angus & Robertson Australia in 1984
A division of HarperCollins Publishers
(Australia) Pty Ltd
Reprinted 1984 (twice), 1985 (three times),
1986 (three times), 1987 (twice), 1988, 1989,
1990, 1991

Angus & Robertson (UK)
77–85 Fulham Palace Road, London W6 8JB
United Kingdom
Collins/Angus & Robertson Publishers Australia
Unit 4, Eden Park, 31 Waterloo Road,
North Ryde, NSW 2113, Australia
William Collins Publishers Ltd
31 View Road, Glenfield, Auckland 10,
New Zealand

in collaboration with
THE MERCIER PRESS LIMITED

4 Bridge Street, Cork, Ireland, and
24 Lower Abbey Street, Dublin 1, Ireland

National Library of Australia
Cataloguing-in-publication data.
More of the world's best Irish jokes
    I. Wit and humour. I. MacHale, Des.
    II. Silvestro, Louis
808.88'2

ISBN 0 207 15069 9

Printed in Great Britain by
BPCC Hazell Books, Aylesbury

Publisher's Note

When we first published *The World's Best Irish Jokes* there was a terrible howl of anguish from those who felt we were being "racist" in raising a laugh at the antics and verbal contortions of our beloved Irish cousins and forebears.

Of course, we are aware that there are many vicious and unsympathetic jokes told against the Irish (and against most other large ethnic groups) but we don't find such jokes funny at all and our humble attempt was intended to be affectionate in mood. We mainly related stories of Irish folk who were warm, gregarious, big-hearted, boozy, genuinely pious, ingenious and, in a weird kind of way, displaying the kind of instinctive creativity characteristic of the intuitive lateral thinker.

Then we heard about Des MacHale, who had published books called *The Official Kerryman Joke Book, The Bumper Book of Kerryman Jokes* and *Irish Love and Marriage Jokes* in Ireland and enjoyed enormous popularity there, selling many thousands of copies. When we came to look at his stories about the people from County Kerry, we discovered that while the rest of the world laughed at the Irish, the Irish themselves laughed at their country cousins, the Kerry people.

Emboldened by this confirmation of what we already knew — that the Irish are perfectly capable of laughing at themselves — we have taken the cream of Des MacHale's Kerryman jokes, translated them into the form the world best knows them in, added a few ring-ins that were just too good to miss, and behold: *More of the World's Best Irish Jokes*.

I was discussing Irish jokes recently with a friend who's a television director and who had just returned from Ireland; he told me the Irish just have a different way with language. He said he'd asked the distance from A to B of some chap in the country, who replied: "Well, sir, it's seven miles. But, for a young chap like you, it'd be only five."

The farmer's words are not merely funny and rather beautiful, but within them there is an essential truth that tantalises the mind. Likewise this collection will both amuse and bemuse you. I hope it leaves you as fond of the Irish people as we are.

♣A Scotsman, an Englishman and an Irishman arrived in Los Angeles too late to buy tickets for the 1984 Olympics. Even the scalpers had nothing to offer.

They were outside the main stadium and the cheers of the crowd were loud in their ears and every so often the tune of a national anthem would blare out as some athletic event was won.

"Well, we've come this far laddies," said the Scot. "I'm not going to be beaten." So saying, he looked around for inspiration and suddenly his eyes lit up. He ran to the car park fenced off with barbed wire held in place with long wooden stakes. He uprooted a stake then stripped down to his singlet and underpants.

His companions watched as, with stake clasped firmly in both hands, he jogged to the competitors' entrance. They heard him say: "McFaddon, pole vault competitor," and watched amazed as he was admitted to the arena.

Inspired, the Englishman looked about; his eyes lighted on the nearby cars. Without hesitation he too stripped to his underwear, grabbed a hub cap from a nearby Buick and, jogging to the entrance, announced himself: "Lincoln, I'm expected for the discus event." He too was admitted.

"Sure now," muttered the Irishman, "three can play at that game." So saying, he stripped to his underpants . . .

The gateman was not deceived. This figure before him, wrapped in barbed wire and dripping blood from the many small cuts it made was not "O'Leary, for the fencing".

Then there was the Irishman who went surf-riding.

His horse drowned.

An Englishman, a Scotsman, and an Irishman were reminiscing on great sporting occasions.

"The closest race I ever saw was a yacht race," said the Englishman, "in which one of the boats, which had been recently painted, won by the breadth of a coat of paint."

"The closest I ever saw," declared the Scotsman, "was one in which a horse, stung by a bee, won by the height of the swelling on his nose."

"The closest race I ever saw," said the Irishman, "is the Scotch."

The Irish skating championships were reaching a climax when the final competitor had a bit of a mishap. He slipped just as he was entering the rink, slid across the floor on his rear end, and demolished the judges' table with his feet.

"Could I have your marks please, just for the record," said the chief official.

"0.0," said the Dublin judge.

"0.0," said the Galway judge.

"0.0," said the Cork judge.

"9.9," said the Kerry judge.

"Hold on a moment," said the chief official to the Kerry judge, "how can you award such a high score for such a terrible performance?"

"Well," said the Kerry judge, "you've got to make allowances — it's as slippery as hell out there."

The Irish Tug-of-War Team?
They were disqualified for pushing.

Two Irishmen were out hunting when one of them saw a rabbit.

"Quick," said the first, "shoot it."

"I can't," said the second, "my gun isn't loaded."

"Well," said the first, "you know that, and I know that, but the rabbit doesn't."

Have you heard about the Irish cricket match that was cancelled because both sides showed up wearing the same colours?

An American tourist travelling in Limerick came across a little antique shop in which he was lucky enough to pick up, for a mere £150, the skull of Brian Boru. Included in the price was a certificate of the skull's authenticity, signed by Brian Boru himself.

Ten years later the tourist returned to Ireland and asked the antique shop owner if he had any more bargains.

"I've got the very thing for you," said the Irishman. "It's the genuine skull of Brian Boru."

"You swindler," said the American. "You sold me that ten years ago," and, producing the skull, added, "Look, they're not even the same size."

"You have it all wrong," said the Irishman. "This is the skull of Brian Boru when he was a lad."

Irish Graffiti No. 1

An Irishman and an American were sitting in the bar at Shannon Airport.

"I've come to meet my brother," said the Irishman. "He's due to fly in from America in an hour's time. It's his first trip home in forty years."

"Will you be able to recognise him?" asked the American.

"I'm sure I won't," said the Irishman, "after all that time."

"I wonder if he will recognise you?" said the American.

"Of course he will," said the Irishman. "Sure, I haven't been away at all."

On the other side of the Irish Sea, two Irishmen were travelling through Dorset when they saw a sign saying: CLEAN REST ROOM AHEAD. So they did.

A young man on a walking holiday in Ireland was out on a wild country road when it began to look like rain. Whether to go on or go back? Fortunately, he came across an old man digging peat and asked him how long it would take to get to the next village.

The old man didn't speak or even look at the lad, so, reshouldering his knapsack, he went on his way. He had only gone a few metres further along the road when the old man hailed him back.

"It will take you twenty minutes," he said with a nod.

"Thanks, but why didn't you tell me before?" asked the lad.

"Because," replied the old man, "I didn't know how fast you could walk."

The famous Irish maze — a rescue service is available for those who get lost inside. Some Irishmen have difficulty finding their way in.

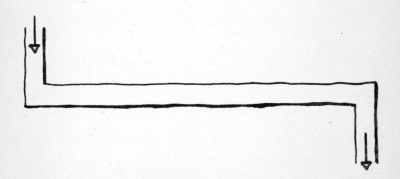

Then there was the tourist in a little Sligo village who noticed that the two clocks on the church tower showed different times.

He asked a local to explain.

"Look," said the Sligoman, "if both clocks showed the same time, we would need only one clock."

An American tourist was being shown around Kerry by a local guide.

"Say, Mac," said the American, "what's that mountain over there?"

"That's Carrantouhill," said the Kerryman. "It's the highest mountain in the world."

"But what about Mount Everest?" said the American.

"Oh, exceptin' those in foreign parts," said the Kerryman.

A tourist walked into a fish and chip shop in Derry.

"I'll have fish and chips twice," he orders.

"Sure, I heard you the first time," came the reply.

Pat: "Er, is that British Airways? Can you tell me how long it takes to fly from Dublin to London?"

Booking clerk: "Just a minute, sir . . ."

Pat: "O.K. Thanks a lot," and he hung up.

Two very seasick Irishmen were returning by boat to Ireland. One said to the other: "Mick, for God's sake ask the captain to stop the ship for a few minutes until I get a rest, or I'll have to get out and walk."

Four good fellows, old friends, met, after many years, in an Irish provincial town. They visited a pub and had several drinks. Then all four left for the railway station. On arrival at the train, three of the four got in and the train pulled out, leaving the fourth fellow standing on the platform, laughing until he was weak.

"What the devil are you laughing at?" asked the station master.

"Sure, they were supposed to be seeing me off."

♣Two Englishmen and two Irishmen travelled regularly to work on the same train and after some time the Englishmen noticed that the Irishmen always used just one ticket between them. When asked to explain, the Irishmen said that when the ticket collector was approaching they always went into the toilet together and passed the one ticket under the door, whereupon it was punched and passed back to them.

Next morning the Englishmen bought one ticket between them and decided to try out the Irishmen's scheme. When they heard the conductor approaching, the two Englishmen got up and quickly locked themselves in the toilet. Moments later the Irishmen followed them and one of the Irishmen knocked on the door, saying: "Tickets please."

When the ticket appeared one of the Irishmen grabbed it and then the two Irishmen, who had bought no tickets at all that day, quickly locked themselves into the toilet opposite.

♣When Patrick was on a visit to Liverpool he met his friend Mike.

"Hello, Paddy, when did you come over?" asked Mike.

"Yesterday," said Paddy.

"And did you come by sea or air?" asked Mike.

"I don't know, you see my wife bought the tickets."

On a small charter flight out of Dublin there are only four passengers. An English businessman, a French priest, an Irishman who is the Brain of Ireland and an Australian mountaineer with his rucksack.

Suddenly the pilot enters the cabin looking white-faced. He apologises for the inconvenience but announces that due to engine failure the plane is about to crash.

"Regrettably there are only four parachutes," he announces, "but I know you'll agree that I should take one so I can report the cause of the crash." So saying, he grabs a 'chute and jumps.

The priest says he has a flock of five thousand souls to look after and he is a very important person to them. He grabs the second parachute and out he jumps.

Then the Brain of Ireland steps forward and says he has to represent Ireland in the Brain of the World competition next month, so for the Old Country's sake he feels he has to take a parachute. So saying, he jumps.

The Englishman turns to the Australian and says:

"Well, old boy, one 'chute left. What do we do now?"

"No worries, mate," says the Aussie, "there are still two 'chutes — the bloody Brain of Ireland took my bloody rucksack."

The great Arctic explorer, Dr Nansen, was giving a lecture on his adventures when an Irishman in the audience interrupted him.

"Sure," bragged Paddy, "Oi've travelled farther north than anybody."

"What nonsense!" exclaimed the doctor, getting angry. "Why, sir, do you know I calculate to have travelled as far as any human being can possibly get."

But still Paddy persisted, and went on to say, "Now, listen to this. How do you know that you've travelled as far as any human being can get?"

"Because," replied Nansen, "I came to a huge wall of ice that no-one could get around."

"What did you do then?"

"Well, I discussed it with my staff and we decided we would have to turn back."

"Ah, yes, begorrah," exclaimed Pat. "Oi heard you. Oi was on the other side of the wall!"

And what about the Irish explorer who paid £10 for a sheet of sandpaper?

He thought it was a map of the Sahara Desert.

One Irish adventurer was telling another about his travels in Africa. "I once saw a man with his hands tied behind his back being beheaded," he told him, "and do you know what happened? He picked up his head and put it back on his shoulders again."

"How could he do that," asked the second Irishman, "when his hands were tied behind his back?"

"You fool," said the first, "couldn't he pick it up with his teeth?"

An Irishman was boasting about his brother's exploits in the Army.

"He was the finest soldier of the day," he claimed. "Although he had only one arm, he used to rush into battle without a single weapon. His favourite method of disposing of the enemy was by banging their heads together."

"How could he bang their heads together if he had only one arm?" asked a listener.

"In the heat of the battle," replied the Irishman, "my brother forgot all about that."

An old Irish Army sergeant wasn't feeling very well so he went to the doctor and had a check-up.

"When did you last have a drink?" the doctor asked him.

"1945," said the sergeant.

"That's a long time without a drink," said the doctor.

"It certainly is," said the sergeant. "It's nearly 2130 now."

The Irish sergeant-major was drilling a squad of new recruits.

"Left, left, left, right, left," he barked. "Right turn," he challenged.

Try as he might, he could not get the recruits to form a straight line once the squad changed direction.

"What's the matter with you," he shouted in exasperation. "Can't you line up at all? That line is as crooked as a corkscrew. All of you fall out and take a look at it."

Paddy Murphy was given leave of absence from his troop, the Cork Fusiliers, the morning after pay day. When he failed to reappear at the end of his leave the military police were sent in search. Eventually Murphy was found and brought before his commanding officer.

"Well, Murphy, you look as if you have been celebrating."

"Yes, sir."

"Have you any money left?"

"No, sir."

"You had £43 when you left the barracks, didn't you man?"

"I did, sir, yes."

"Well, what did you do with it?"

"Well, sir, I was walking along and I met an old, old friend and we went into a saloon to celebrate our reunion and I spent £10. Then we came out and were walking along and I met another old friend. Well, we had to celebrate our meeting too so we went into another saloon and I spent another £10. And then I came out and we met another old friend. Well, sir, you can't let these golden opportunities slip so we did more celebrating and I spent another £10. Then, just as we came out of that pub we ran into another old friend. Sure, I hadn't seen him for a terrible long time so we all just slipped back into the saloon and I spent another £10. And it was sometime after that that the MPs arrived."

"But man, that makes only £40. What did you do with the other £3?" Murphy thought. Then he shook his head sadly and said:

"I can't work it out sir, I reckon I must have squandered that money foolishly."

The drill sergeant was almost at his wits' end. He had to get his Irish recruits through bayonet practice, but the weather was so hot all they could manage was a listless jab at the stuffed dummies and a weak mewling that had little in common with the full-throated roar of a war-cry.

Then inspiration struck.

"Right-oh boys, stop the drill! Now listen. Those there aren't just dummies, they're your enemy. Last night, it was, they burned your home down to the very ground, they killed your parents and raped your sisters. The blood ran thick and strong like a river and the cries of the young were pitiful to hear. But they paid no heed. They robbed you of all your money and they drank all the whisky in the place. Now men, what are you going to do about it?"

With a roar the line of soldiers sprang forward toward the dummies. Bayonets gleamed and faces were grim. One lad looked particularly fierce but he stopped in his tracks to ask:

"Sure, and which of these bastards was it drank the whisky, sergeant?"

"Is this soldier dangerously wounded?" an Irish doctor was asked.

"Two of the wounds are fatal," he replied, "but the third can be cured, provided the patient gets a few weeks' rest."

An Irishman joined the American Air Force and was making his first parachute jump. The instructor said, "When you jump out of the plane, shout 'Geronimo' and pull the rip-cord."

When the Irishman woke up in hospital a few days later the first thing he said was, "What was the name of that Indian again?"

"What's he mean by 'Halt', Mike?" Paddy asked of his mate and fellow recruit as they were being drilled on their first day of army training.

"Why," said Mike, "when he says 'Halt', you just bring the foot that's on the ground to the side of the foot that's in the air, and remain motionless."

The plane was circling at five thousand metres and the Killarney Green Berets paratroop squad were about to make their first jump.

"Hold everything!" shouted the commanding officer. "You're not wearing your parachute, O'Leary."

"It's all right, sir," replied O'Leary. "Sure, it's only a practice jump we're doing."

The sergeant had just finished his two-hour lecture on a soldier's duty and, looking at the sea of different faces, he wondered if his message had penetrated at all and whether it would be remembered. So, turning to one of them he asked: "Now then, Private O'Grady, why should a soldier be ready to die for his country?"

The Irishman scratched his head for a while, then an enlightened smile flitted across his face. "Sure, sir," he said pleasantly, "you're quite right. Why should he?"

And you'll remember also the Irishman who got a job as a doorman in a big building. He managed very well with the PUSH and PULL signs but he was seen struggling with his fingers under a door marked LIFT.

Meanwhile his brother it was who got a job at an observatory. During his first night's duty he paused to watch a learned professor who was peering through a large telescope. Just then a star fell.

"Man alive!" exclaimed the astonished Irishman. "You're a fine shot."

🍀 Seen in a Wexford beauty parlour:

EARS PIERCED
WHILE YOU WAIT

🍀 Paddy was telling Mick of his plans to make a lot of money.

"I intend to buy a dozen swarms of bees and every morning at dawn I'm going to let them into the park opposite my house to spend all day making honey, while I relax."

"But the park doesn't open until nine o'clock," protested Mick.

"I realise that," said Paddy, "but I know where there is a hole in the fence."

On a building site one of the workers caught his head between some pipes and lost both his ears. After some time in hospital he returned to work. Meanwhile the foreman had been going round to all the workers telling them the lad with no ears, Henry by name, was terribly sensitive about it and no-one was to mention it.

On Henry's first day back, Paddy goes up to him.

"Great to see you back Henry. But, for goodness sake, how is it you've given up wearing glasses?"

Pat: "I've just bought one of those new silicon chip hearing aids — it's so small you can hardly see it."

Mick: "That's terrific — does it work well?"

Pat: "Half past seven."

Seen in a Kildare auctioneers:

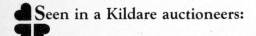

THE HIGHEST BIDDER
TO BE THE PURCHASER
UNLESS SOMEBODY BIDS MORE

" ♣Pat, if Mr Jones comes back before I return, tell him that I will meet him at two o'clock."

"All right, sir; but what shall I tell him if he doesn't come?"

♣Denis was working on the Waterford to Cork railway line, when suddenly a train came speeding along the line. He took off down the track but was knocked down and badly injured. When he regained consciousness in hospital, the doctor asked him why he had not run up the embankment.

"Don't be a fool," said Denis, "if I couldn't out-run it on the flat, what chance had I running uphill?"

But have you heard about Michael Flynn? Out of work he was when he went on board a vessel and asked the captain if he could give him a job.

"Well," grinned the captain, handing Michael a bit of rope, "if you can find four ends to that rope, you're hired."

"Four ends, your honour! Well, now," and he showed one end of the rope, "there's one end."

"That's right."

He took hold of the other end, and held it out. "And there's two ends — right?"

"Exactly."

"And one end and two ends make three ends, right?"

The captain laughed. "But I said four."

With a quick movement Michael threw the rope into the harbour. "There's an end to the whole rope, sir — and three ends and one more end makes four ends!"

He got the job.

Pat bet Mike that he could carry a full hod of bricks to the top of a five-storey building, with Mike sitting on top of the hod. When near the top, Pat tripped, almost fell and nearly dropped Mike to the pavement below.

Arriving at the top, Pat puffed, "Begorrah, I've won the bet."

"Sure," said Mike sadly. "But when ye slipped, I was sure I had ye."

The midday whistle had blown when Murphy shouted, "Has anyone seen me vest?"

"Sure, Murphy," said Pat, "and you've got it on."

"Right and I have," replied Murphy, gazing solemnly at his bosom, "and it's a good thing you saw it or I'd have gone home without it."

Then there were the two Irishmen painting a house.

Pat: "Have you got a good hold on that paint brush, Mick?"

Mick: "Yes I have, Pat. Why?"

Pat: "Well, hold on tight because I'm taking this ladder away."

Timothy O'Leary bought Sean Casey's sorrel mare for £100 cash. Tim got to thinking that since Sean paid the price so willingly, the mare must be worth more. Next day he bought the mare back for £200. Later Sean again bought the mare — for £300. This kept going on until the price went up to £1,500.

Then a Limerick horse trader came on the scene and bought the horse from Sean for £2,000.

Hearing of this, Tim hurried over to Sean and berated him:

"You are a fool, selling that mare. Both of us were making a good living off her!"

Pat and Mick each had a horse, but they couldn't tell them apart. So Pat cut the tail off his horse, and all went well for a while. But then Mick's horse lost its tail in an accident, so they were back where they started. Finally, they consulted a wise man in the village where they lived and he said: "Can't you two fools see that the black horse is three centimetres taller than the white horse?"

Paddy went to a riding stable and hired a horse. "Hold on for a moment," said the assistant as he helped him onto the horse, "aren't you putting that saddle on backwards?"

"You don't even know which way I want to go."

Dinny and Dave, farmers, met one day at a Kilkenny fair.

"Tell me," said Dinny, "what did you give your mule when he had colic?"

"Turpentine," said Dave.

A few months later they met again.

"What did you say you gave your mule when he had colic?" asked Dinny.

"Turpentine," said Dave.

"Well, I gave my mule turpentine, and he died," said Dinny.

"So did mine," said Dave, "so did mine."

Pat's cat was feeling out of sorts so Pat called in the vet.

"There's nothing really the matter with your cat," said the vet. "It's all perfectly natural, she's going to have kittens."

"That's impossible," said Pat, "she's a prize-winning cat and I've never let her out of my sight for a moment. She's never been near a tom cat in her life."

"How about him over there?" asked the vet, pointing to a big tom cat sitting on a couch smiling to himself.

"Don't be ridiculous," said Pat, "that's her brother."

What does an Irishman call his pet zebra?
Spot.

Two Irishmen were walking down the street when one turned to the other and said, "Look, there's a dead pigeon."

"Where? Where?" said the second Irishman, looking up at the sky.

Pat was out for a ride on his donkey when the animal took fright, bolted and finally wound up with one of his hind legs caught in one of the stirrups.

"Hold on a minute," said Pat. "If you're getting on then I'm getting off."

An Englishman and an Irishman were sharing a railway carriage and the Englishman had with him a large dog.

"What sort of dog is that?" asked the Irishman.

"It's a cross between an Irishman and an ape," said the Englishman.

"In that case," said the Irishman, "it's related to both of us."

Circus Owner: "You left the door of the lion's cage open all night last night."

Mick: "What matter, sure nobody in his senses would bother stealing a lion."

Pat followed his friend Mick's example and left Ireland to work in England. Though they had since lost contact, Mick had mentioned how easy it was to get a job at Whipsnade Open Zoo. So Pat applied. Unfortunately they had no keeper's jobs available. There was not even the position of a sweeper vacant.

"But I tell you what, Pat," the manager said, "the gorilla died a couple of days ago — and what's a zoo without a gorilla. But we've kept his pelt entire. Now, if you crawl into that skin and take over his enclosure we'll feed and house you and pay you handsomely as well."

Pat had a look over the lovely field that was the gorilla enclosure. He surveyed the comfortable gorilla house and tested the bed provided. He agreed to take on the job.

Very soon Pat had become a great favourite with visitors to the zoo. Being a bit of an extrovert, he would always put on a good act — tumbling, chest-thumping and growling. But the climax of his performance was most popular. Whenever there was a good crowd, Pat would scale a large oak tree at the side of his enclosure where it adjoined the lions' range. He would then climb out on a limb overhanging the lions' pen, and pelt the lion and lionesses with acorns. The big-maned lion in particular would roar with rage and stamp about and the crowd would roar with delight.

One public holiday a particularly large crowd had gathered, and Pat was aloft and reaching the peak of his performance. He had just finished off the acorn pelting with a bit of chest-thumping when the branch he was balanced on broke. He fell to the ground at the lion's feet.

Pat jumped up shouting for help and was about to scarper when the lion whispered:

"Hold yer tongue, Pat. Sure do yer want to lose us the best jobs we've ever had?"

Irish Graffiti No. 2

There's no point voting
in elections
-the government always
wins anyway

For many years Old Dinny McGuinness had been due to go into hospital for an operation, so he finally plucked up the courage. As soon as he arrived at the hospital he was given a thorough bath.

"Well," he said to himself, "thank goodness that's over, I've been dreading that operation for years."

A fellow was explaining to Michael Murphy how nature sometimes compensates for a person's deficiences.

"For example," he told him, "if a man is deaf, he may have keener sight, and if a man is blind, he may have a very keen sense of smell."

"I think I see what you mean," said Michael, "I've often noticed that if a man has one short leg, then the other one is always a little bit longer."

Then there was Barry O'Loughlin who went to the doctor to get some medicine as he wasn't feeling very well.

"This is pretty strong stuff," said the doctor, "so take some the first day, then skip a day, take some again and then skip another day and so on."

A few months later the doctor met Barry's wife and asked her how he was.

"Oh, he's dead," she told him.

"Didn't the medicine I prescribed do him any good?" asked the doctor.

"Oh, the medicine was fine," she replied. "It was all that skipping that killed him."

Mrs Casey accompanied her daughter Kathleen to her appointment with Dr Flynn and explained the situation.

"Sure, she's been having some strange symptoms and it's worried about her I am."

Dr Flynn examined Kathleen carefully then announced, "Sure, it's pregnant your daughter is."

"Saints preserve us," gasped Mrs Casey. "Will you be listening to the great spalpeen. My daughter pregnant! I've never heard such nonsense, indeed I haven't," and she turned confidently to Kathleen for confirmation.

Kathleen blushed and replied with every vestige of great modesty, "No, no, of course not. Why, I've never even kissed a man!"

Flynn looked from mother to daughter and back again. Then, silently he stood up and walked to the window. He stared out and continued to stare with apparently great concentration.

Finally Mrs Casey could stand it no longer and was compelled to ask, "Doctor, is there something wrong out there?"

"No," said Flynn. "Sure, it's just that the last time anything like this happened, a star appeared in the East and I was looking to see if another one was going to show up at all. Three fellows showed up with gifts of gold, frankincense and myrrh and I don't want to miss them this time."

Brendan Kelly, superintendent of a hospital for the disabled, was one day showing a millionaire round the place in the hope of getting a large donation from him. So he took him into a ward where there was a man with no arms.

"That's dreadful," said the millionaire. "Look, here's a cheque for £50,000."

Brendan thought he would squeeze a little more money out of him, so he took him into a ward where there was a man with neither arms nor legs.

"That's terrible," said the millionaire. "I'll increase that to £100,000."

Never one to miss a good opportunity, Brendan decided to squeeze just a little more money out of his benefactor, so he took him to a ward where there was a bed with just a single tooth lying on the pillow.

"Oh my God," gasped the millionaire, "is that all that's left of the poor fellow?"

"Worse still," said Brendan, "he's having it out tomorrow."

A customer went into Denis O'Brien's shop and asked to buy some mustard.

"I don't have any in the shop," said Denis, "but I have some in the store; come with me and pick out the kind of mustard you want."

As they went through the store the customer couldn't help noticing bag after bag of salt on the shelves.

"You must sell an awful lot of salt," he remarked.

"I sell very little salt," replied Denis, "but the fellow who sells me salt, boy, can he sell salt."

Did you hear about the Irishman who spent an hour in a big store looking for a cap with a peak at the back?

Then there was the Irishman who was stranded for an hour in a supermarket when the escalator broke down.

Sign in a Dublin shop:

NO DISSATISFIED
CUSTOMER
IS EVER ALLOWED
TO LEAVE THE SHOP

An Irishman got a job as a lumberjack, but try as he might, he couldn't meet his quota of fifty trees a day. By chance he saw an advertisement in a shop window for chain saws "guaranteed to fell sixty trees a day". So he bought one, but the best he could manage was forty trees a day.

He took it back to the shop and complained that there must be something wrong with it.

"Let me look at it," said the man in the shop and, taking the chain saw, he switched it on.

"What's that noise?" said the Irishman.

When Dave Doyle was applying for a credit card the manager of the credit card company asked him if he had much money in the bank.

"I have," said Dave.

"How much?" asked the manager.

"I don't know exactly," said Dave, "I haven't shaken it lately."

An Irishman went into a post office and asked if there were any letters for him.

"I'll see sir," said the clerk. "What is your name?"

"You're having me on now because I'm Irish," said the Irishman. "Won't you see the name on the envelope."

"Mrs Flanagan," said the landlord, "I've decided to raise your rent."

"Ah, now," beamed Mrs Flanagan. "It's the darling you certainly are. I was wondering how I could raise it myself, sir."

An Irishman had just been found guilty of a serious crime and the judge asked him if he could pay anything at all towards costs which had also been awarded against him.

"Not a penny your honour," said the accused. "Everything I own I've given to my lawyer and three of the jury."

Two Irishmen escaped from gaol and were being followed by the police with tracker dogs. The two decided to climb up into the trees in order to escape. As the dogs came sniffing at the base of the tree where the first escapee was hiding he went, "miaow, miaow".

"Come away," said the policeman, "that's only a cat."

The dogs then began to sniff at the base of the tree where the second was hiding.

"Moo, moo," went the second Irishman.

NEWSFLASH!!
Thieves escaped with over half a million pounds from a Galway bank last night.

Police are baffled trying to figure out the motive for the crime.

A Dubliner was in court charged with parking his car in a restricted area. The judge asked him if he had anything to say in his defence.

"They shouldn't put up such misleading notices," said the Dubliner. "It said, FINE FOR PARKING HERE."

Paddy was sent to gaol and was sharing a cell with two others.

"What are you in for?" he asked the first.

"Stealing a few bales of straw," he replied.

"And how long did you get?" asked Paddy.

"Six months," he replied.

"And what are you in for?" Paddy asked the second.

"Rape," he replied.

"And how long did you get?"

"Seven years," he replied.

"Heavens above," said Paddy, "you must have stolen a whole hectare of it."

A dangerous criminal had escaped, so the police issued the usual photographs: left profile, front view, and right profile. A few days later they received the following telegram from an Irish detective:

"Have captured the fellow on the left, and the fellow in the middle, and at the rate I'm going it won't be long before I get the fellow on the right as well."

Paddy and Mick were sent to gaol in a high security prison, but they developed an ingenious method of communicating with each other by means of a secret code and banging on the pipes.

However, their scheme broke down when they were transferred to different cells.

CROSSWORD FOR IRISHMEN

CLUES:
1. (Across) The indefinite article (anagram).
1. (Down) The first letter of the alphabet.

An Englishman asked an Irishman to show him the biggest building in an Irish town.

"There it is now," said the Irishman, "isn't it a fine structure entirely?"

"Is that your biggest building?" asked the Englishman. "Why, back in England we have buildings over a hundred times the size of that."

"I'm not surprised," said the Irishman, "that's the local lunatic asylum."

An English politician was speaking on a platform. "I was born an Englishman," he shouted, "I have lived all my life an Englishman, and I hope to die an Englishman."

"Have you no ambition?" shouted Pat from the audience.

At another political rally the Tory speaker was also having trouble.

"Rah for Ireland!" yelled Pat.

"Rah for hell!" roared a disgusted Tory.

"Everyone for his own country!" came back Pat.

Two Irishmen, one very fat and the other very thin, once decided to fight a duel with pistols. Their seconds decided that the thin man had an unfair advantage because of the bigger target that the fat man presented. Finally they agreed that the figure of the thin man be chalked on the body of the fat man and that any bullets hitting the fat man outside the line would not count.

Lecturer: "Here is a list of statistics about Donegal farmers broken down by age and sex."

Voice from the back: "What about the drink?"

It was a disillusioned Irishman who decided to leave England, where he had lived for twenty years, and return to his native country.

"Sure," he explained, "in the reign of Henry the Eighth homosexuality was punishable by death. Later it merited just a term of imprisonment. Recently it was made legal. I'm getting out before they make it compulsory."

With too many ales under their belts, a couple of Englishmen decided to pick a fight with the Irishman who was a regular at their London pub.

"Just watch this, Charles," said one. "I'll make him so hopping mad he'll have to hit me and start the fight," and he wandered over to Paddy.

"Listen here, my man," he said in a lofty tone, "do you know St Patrick?"

"Yes sir, certainly. Well not to say know him personally but I know of him, certainly, sir," said Paddy.

"Well, you'll know then that he was a moron," the Englishman went on.

"No, sir," said Pat politely. "No, I didn't know that. That's certainly interesting though. A moron you say."

"Not only that," the Englishman continued, slightly disconcerted by the lack of a desired response, "not only that, but St Patrick was a shithead as well."

"You don't say, sir," replied Paddy. "Well, you live and learn, don't you, sir."

The Englishman gave up and went back to his ale. His friend Charles, who had heard the baiting, sprang to his feet.

"Leave it to me, I'll make him mad," he said, and weaved his way to Paddy's side.

"Listen here," he said to Paddy, "did you know St Patrick was an Englishman?"

"So your friend was just telling me, sir."

An Irishman and a Scot were heatedly arguing about the antiquity of their races and the merits of their families.

"I tell ye laddie," bragged the Scot, "I'm sprung from the best stock in the world — from the stock of the kings of Scotland. I've got royal blood in my veins. An' what stock are ye sprung from?"

"I come from the Caseys," said the Irishman simply. "They never sprung from nobody — they sprung at 'em!"

Then an Englishman joined the battle and, turning to the Scot, he asked: "What would you be were you not a Scot!"

The Scot said: "Why, an Englishman, of course!"

Then the Englishman turned to the gentleman from Ireland and asked him: "And what would you be were you not Irish?"

Casey thought a moment and said: "I'd be ashamed of meself!"

An Irishman went to confession in London. "Bless me father for I have sinned — I've blown up a ten kilometre stretch of track belonging to British Rail."

"For your penance my son," said the Irish priest, "do the stations."

That same priest got into trouble with his continual preaching of anti-English sermons. Eventually, he was given a final warning and told that if he made even a single anti-English reference in a future sermon he would be suspended. One day the bishop sneaked incognito into the church where the priest was preaching. This is what he heard:

And the Lord said to Peter, "Will you betray me?"

And Peter replied, "No, Lord, I will not betray you."

And the Lord said to John, "Will you betray me?"

And John replied, "No, Lord, I will not betray you."

And the Lord said to Judas, "Will you betray me?"

And Judas replied, "Not bloomin' likely, mate, I'm yer friend, ain't I?"

Irish Graffiti No. 3

Thank god I'm an atheist

Pat Bourke, the Tipperary horse dealer, was called from his office by his assistant to help deal with a customer; one Brian O'Leary. Brian, it appeared, had bought an old bay horse, and wanted it shot.

"Shot, sir?" asked Pat.

"Yes, shot," replied Brian with fervour.

"Well, Mick," said the dealer to his assistant. "You know our policy. The customer is always right."

So the horse was shot.

"Now that's done, sir, what shall we do with it?" asked Pat.

"Well I want it delivered to my home tomorrow," Brian instructed, and he gave them the address.

"Till tomorrow then, sir," said Pat, trying not to look too puzzled.

The next day a big van rolled up to Brian O'Leary's front door. Pat and three others got out and unloaded the dead horse.

"Now, bring it inside," Brian directed, waving them in the front door.

"Inside, sir, certainly, sir," said Pat, looking intrigued but not daring to question a customer.

"Yes, bring it in, men, and take it upstairs."

"Upstairs, sir, certainly."

"Yes, now take it into the bathroom."

"The bathroom, sir, certainly."

"Yes, now sit it on the lavatory."

"That was 'sit it on the lavatory' wasn't it, sir? Yes sir, certainly," and the men arranged the old dead nag so that it sat sagging over the Fowlerware.

This was all too much for Pat. His curiosity could no longer be contained.

"Tell me, sir, I beg of you, what's it all about? You've bought a horse, had it shot, had it delivered to your home, had it taken inside, upstairs and sat on the lavatory. In the name of all that's holy, why?"

"Well," said Brian, "my wife Bridget is a woman who knows everything. Everything I say she says 'I know' even before I've finished saying it. Just once I want to get in first. So when Bridget comes home from her mother's today, she'll go upstairs, go into the bathroom and then she'll come running down to me to say 'there's a dead horse sitting on the lavatory' and I'll say 'I know'."

Pat went to confession and when he had confessed his sins he was told by the priest to say the Our Father for his penance.

"I'm afraid I don't know that prayer," said Pat.

"How about the Hail Mary?" said the priest.

"I don't know that either," said Pat.

"Is there any prayer you do know?" asked the priest.

"Yes," said Pat, "there's the Angelus."

"Well, you can say that if you like," said the priest.

"Boing, boing, boing," said Pat.

An Englishman on holiday in Ireland for the first time was warned by his Irish wife to be discreet in his remarks about religion, and not to make any insulting remarks about Catholics in particular.

One evening the Englishman was in a pub playing darts when the television programme was interrupted to announce that the Pope was seriously ill. All the other players gathered round the set to get more details.

"Look," said the Englishman, "let's get on with the darts game, and to hell with the Pope."

When he regained consciousness in hospital a few days later, his wife said:

"I thought I told you not to make any insulting remarks about Catholics."

"Nobody told me the Pope was a Catholic," said the Englishman.

While on his parish rounds, Father O'Brien sees three children playing together — two small strangers and Michael O'Conner, one of his flock. He stops, is introduced and, thinking of priestly duties, tells the children he'll give £2 to whoever can answer the question, "Who was the greatest man on earth?"

The boys think for a minute and one of the strangers, Mark Bunyan, bursts out: "President Kennedy."

"Sure now," says the priest, "he was a good man all right, but not the greatest. Come now, Michael," he prompts, "you should know this if you remember your catechism."

"Well, Father," says Michael, "I'd say it was St Patrick because he brought Christianity to Ireland."

"No, Michael. It's a good answer, but not the right one," says the priest, and he confidently repockets the £2.

But Isaac Goldstein, the other stranger, pipes up: "It was Jesus Christ."

The priest pays up, but with a puzzled air. "Isaac," he asks, "surely someone of your faith doesn't believe that?"

"Oh no, Father. I know Moses was the greatest. But business is business."

Have you heard about the Irishman who thought that a transistor was a nun who wore men's clothes?

Maureen was attending her convent school reunion where the Reverend Mother was asking each of her ex-pupils what career she had chosen.

"I've become a prostitute," said one, and the Reverend Mother promptly fainted.

When she was revived she asked the girl what she had said.

"A prostitute," repeated the girl.

"Thank Heavens," said the Reverend Mother, "I thought for a moment you had said a Protestant."

While crossing St Peter's Square on a wet and gusty evening, his collar turned up against the wind, Patrick suddenly clutched at his chest and collapsed in a puddle on the ground.

Luckily, friends were close at hand and immediately rushed to his aid.

"Quick," said Patrick, "get me a rabbi."

"But, Patrick, you're a good Irish Catholic boy."

"Ah sure, sure," was the reply, "but I wouldn't dream of bringing His Holiness out on a night like this!"

AN IRISHMAN TYING HIS SHOELACE

A young Irish girl went to church for confession, and said to the priest: "Oh, Father, Father, I have sinned grievously. On Monday night I slept with Sean. On Tuesday night I slept with Patrick, and on Wednesday night I slept with Mick. Oh Father, Father, what shall I do?"

"My child, my child," replied the priest, "go home and squeeze the juice from a whole lemon and drink it."

"Oh, Father, Father, will this purge me of my sin?" she asked.

"No child, but it will take the smile off your face."

Saloonkeeper: "Here, you haven't paid for that whisky you ordered."

Irishman: "What's that you say?"

Saloonkeeper: "I said you haven't paid for that whisky you ordered."

Irishman: "Did you pay for it?"

Saloonkeeper: "Of course I did."

Irishman: "Well, then, what's the good of both of us paying for it?"

Irish barmaid: "I'm sorry, sir, the bar will not be open for half an hour — would you like a drink while you're waiting?"

O'Leary's wife awoke in the small hours to hear him stealthily moving things about in the kitchen.

"What might you be lookin' for?" she asked.

"Nothing," said O'Leary, "just nothing."

"Then ye'll find it in the bottle where the whisky used to be."

An Irishman who was rather too fond of strong drink was asked by the parish priest: "My son, how do you expect to get into heaven?"

The Irishman replied:

"Sure, and that's easy! When I get to the gates of Heaven I'll open the door and shut the door, and open the door and shut the door, and keep on doing that till St Peter gets impatient and says, 'For goodness' sake, Mike, either come in or stay out!'"

An American in a pub bet Joseph Duffy £50 that he couldn't drink ten pints of stout in ten minutes.

"You're on," said Joseph, "give me a few minutes to prepare myself," and he vanished out the door.

Fifteen minutes later he returned and drank the ten pints of stout in ten minutes.

"I knew I could manage it," Joseph exulted, "because I just did it in the pub next door."

An English M.P. was once accosted by a distinctly drunk Irishman in the lobby of the House of Commons.

"Sir," said the Irishman, "you're a fool."

"Sir," retorted the Englishman, "you're drunk."

"I may be," replied the Irishman, "but I'll be sober tomorrow, and you'll still be a fool."

Two poteen makers were discussing their business.

"When I take my stuff into town to sell," explained one, "I always drive very slow, very slow. Maybe only twenty miles an hour."

"What, scared of the Guarda, Pat?"

"No. I've got to age the stuff."

A fellow walked into a bar in London and asked the barman if he had heard the latest Irish joke.

"I'm warning you," said the barman, "I'm an Irishman myself."

"That's all right," said the fellow, "I'll tell it slowly."

Sean Dooley was drinking too much, so his local parish priest persuaded him to join the Pioneer Total Abstinence Association. About a week later the parish priest observed Sean staggering out of a pub.

"I thought you were a Pioneer now," said the priest.

"I am," said Sean, "but not a bigoted one."

An Irish toast:

Saint Patrick was a gentleman,
   Who, thro' strategy and stealth,
Drove all the snakes from Ireland —
   Here's a bumper to his health.
But not too many bumpers,
   Lest we lose ourselves, and then
Forget the good Saint Patrick,
   And see the snakes again.

How do you make a Kerry cocktail? Take a half glass of whisky and add it to another half glass of whisky.

Pat was determined to pass his favourite tavern on his way home and not go in as usual. As he approached it he became somewhat shaky, but, "You can do it, you can do it," he said to himself. And he plucked up all his courage and passed it.

He was about fifty metres beyond it when he turned, saying to himself: "Well done, Pat, me boy. Come back and I'll treat you."

"**F**aith, it's myself had a queer dream now. I dreamt I was in Rome, and that I called upon His Reverence the Pope. I had hardly knocked at the door when His Holiness himself opened it. 'Ah, Pat,' says he, 'is it you that are come to see me?' 'Faith, your honour, and it's nobody else.' 'Come upstairs with me,' he cried. And sure, there was the handsomest room as ever you clapped eyes on. 'Be seated, now,' said His Reverence, 'and what will you be taking?' I was bothered for the moment, but I just said, 'A drop of the cratur,' when he turns to me and says, 'Shall it be hot or cold?' 'Hot,' says I, and away went His Holiness to fetch the hot water, and before he came back I awoke. Arrah! What a fool I was I didn't have it cold."

Ted Mulligan was in court charged with stealing a cow.

"How do you plead?" asked the judge.

"Not guilty," answered Ted.

"Is this the first time you've been up before me?" asked the judge.

"I don't know," said Ted, "what time do you get up at?"

"No," said the judge, "I mean is this the first time you've been in court?"

"Yes," said Ted, "I've never stolen anything before."

The court erupted with laughter so the judge shouted, "Order, order."

"I'll have a pint," said Mulligan.

Have you heard about the Irishman who took his girlfriend into the Tunnel of Love?

They got down to work right away and by the time they came out they had developed three films.

Pat was 150 centimetres tall while Bridget was 180 centimetres, but some fellows will go to any lengths. One night when they were walking by the old forge he asked for a kiss and Bridget consented. So he stood on an old anvil and gave her a little kiss. They walked on and after a few kilometres he asked her for another kiss.

"No," she replied haughtily, "I've given you all the kisses you're going to get for tonight."

"In that case," said Pat in disgust, "I'm not going to carry this anvil one step further."

Bridget's father: "Do you think you could support my daughter if you married her?"

Pat: "Yes sir."

Bridget's father: "Have you ever seen her eat?"

Pat: "Yes sir."

Bridget's father: "Have you ever seen her eat when there's nobody looking?"

" **N**ame even one thing," said Pat in the course of a heated argument with Bridget, "in which you will admit that my family scores over your family."

"Your in-laws are better than my in-laws," said Bridget.

"**H**ow are you getting on with your wife Bridget?" Pat was asked.

"Well," he replied, "sometimes she's better and sometimes she's worse. But from the way she carries on when she's better, I think she's better when she is worse."

One day Pat comes home to find Bridget in bed with a stranger. He goes straight past them to the drawer, pulls out a gun, cocks it and points it at his head.

Bridget says, "For God's sake Patrick, put that gun down."

He says, "Shut yer mouth woman, you're next!"

One morning Pat received a letter in the post warning him "If you don't send £5,000 to the above address immediately, we will kidnap your wife Bridget and you will never see her again."

Pat sent the following reply:

"Dear Sir,

I haven't got £5,000, but your offer interests me greatly."

Incidentally, did you hear about the Irish kidnapper?

He enclosed a stamped self-addressed envelope with the ransom note.

Casey: "Pat has been married five years, but sorra the chick or child has he got."

Cassidy: "True. I wonder is that hereditary in his family or hers."

The phone rang in the maternity hospital and an excited voice at the other end of the line said, "Send an ambulance quickly, my wife Bridget is about to have a baby!"

"Calm down," replied the nurse. "Tell me, is this her first baby?"

"No," said Pat, "this is her husband Pat speaking."

"Well, Pat, do the twins make much noise nights?"

"Noise! Sure, each one cries so loud you can't hear the other."

Pat and Bridget's little five-year-old boy Billy was talking with the little boy next door.

"What age are you?" Billy asked him.

"I don't know," the little fellow replied.

"Do women bother you?" asked Billy.

"No," said the little fellow.

"Then you're four," said Billy.

Pat and Bridget had seventeen children so the Vatican decided to present them with a gold medal struck specially in their honour. The Papal Nuncio delivered the medal in person and told them that they were a credit to the Catholic Church.

"There must be some mistake," said Pat. "We're Protestants."

"Oh my God," said the Papal Nuncio, "don't tell me we've minted a gold medal for two sex-crazy Protestants."

Pat, who had worked for twenty years as the skipper of a boat, fell overboard and was drowned. After the funeral a friend of Bridget's asked the inevitable question— "Did he leave you much?"

"He did indeed," said Bridget, "nearly £20,000."

"Isn't that wonderful," said the friend, "and him that couldn't read or write."

"Or swim," said Bridget.

Two Irishmen were out walking together, when they saw a lorry pass by laden with grassy sods of earth for the laying of a lawn.

"Do you know, Mick," said one of them to the other, "if I ever get rich that's what I'll have done — send away my lawn to be cut."

Mick Murphy got a job as an assistant gardener at a big country house. One day he saw a bird bath for the first time.

"What's that for?" he asked the head gardener.

"That's a bird bath," he replied.

"I don't believe you," said Mick. "There isn't a bird in creation who can tell the difference between Saturday night and any other night of the week."

Bridget lay in bed on the first night of their honeymoon while Pat sat fully clothed on an armchair in the bedroom.

"Why don't you come to bed?" Bridget asked him.

"My mother told me that this would be the most exciting night of my life," said Pat, "and I don't want to miss any of it by going to sleep."

A fellow wanted to have his house renovated, but thought that all the estimates he received were too high. Finally he consulted an Irish building contractor who came to view his house.

"I'll completely redecorate your bedroom for £15," said the Irishman.

"Great," said the fellow, "all the others wanted at least £100."

At this the Irishman rushed over to the window and shouted out "Green side up, green side up."

"How about the bathroom?" asked the fellow. "The others wanted at least £250."

"My men and I will do it for £38.57," said the Irishman, whereupon he rushed to the window and shouted "Green side up, green side up."

"Well you seem to be the man I've been looking for," said the fellow. "Just tell me one thing — why do you go to the window and shout 'Green side up, green side up?'"

"That's just technical information to my workmen," said the Irishman. "They're laying a lawn next door."

An Irishman was planting shade trees when a passing lady said: "You're digging out the holes, are you, Mr Haggerty?"

"No, mum. Oi'm digging out the dirt and leaving the holes."

Seen on a Kildare gravestone:

Here lies John Higley,
whose father and mother
were drowned
on their passage from America.
Had both lived,
they would have been
buried here.

A dead Irishman lay smiling in his coffin. His wife explained to a friend, "He's smiling because he died in his sleep and he doesn't know he's dead yet. He's dreaming he's still alive, so when he wakes up and finds he's dead the shock will kill him."

Passing a cemetery one day, an Irishman paused at a startling inscription on a tombstone. He read the words: "I still live."

After scratching his head in puzzlement for a moment, the Irishman exclaimed: "Bejabbers, if I was dead I'd be honest enough to own up to it!"

In a little Irish village the coroner was addressing the jury when summing up in a suicide case. "If you believe beyond reasonable doubt," he told them, "that the deceased did shoot himself with a gun, then it is your duty in law to return a verdict of *felo de se*."

The jury was out about four hours and when they returned the foreman said, "We agree that the deceased did shoot himself with a gun, but if the coroner claims he fell in the sea we return a verdict of accidentally drowned."

Mick: "What do you charge for a funeral notice in your paper?"
Editor: "Fifty cents a centimetre."
Pat: "Good heavens! And me poor brother was almost two metres high."

When Pat emigrated to America one of the first sights he saw was a dead millionaire being buried. The millionaire was dressed in a mohair suit and was encased in a golden coffin studded with diamonds.

"Now that," said Pat, "is what I call really living."

It was a wet stormy day when Mike buried his wife Kathleen. Just as the funeral party left the graveyard there was a bright flash of lightning and a loud rumble of thunder. Pat looked up at the sky and commented: "She's arrived up there already."

Casey and Riley were working on a building site when one of them fell 20 metres from the scaffolding.

"Are you dead?" asked Casey.

"Yes," replied Riley.

"You're such a liar, I don't know whether to believe you or not," said Casey.

"That proves I'm dead, because if I was alive you'd never have the nerve to call me a liar," said Riley.

Irish Graffiti No. 4

ABOLISH HIRE EDUCATION

When Pat died, Bridget went to a draper's shop to buy him a shroud. Being a practical woman the first question she asked was the price.

"The cost is £5, madam," said the draper.

"But I can get one down the street for £4," protested Bridget.

"Those ones are no good, madam," said the draper. "The corpse would have his knees through it in a week."

The captain of a ship told the mate, an Irishman, of course, to proceed to room thirty-six and arrange to have the occupant, who had died during the night, buried at sea.

An hour later the mate reported, "I proceeded to room twenty-six and had the occupant buried at sea, as requested sir."

"My God," said the captain, "I said room thirty-six. Who was the occupant of room twenty-six?"

"An Englishman, sir."

"Was he dead?"

"Well, he said he wasn't. But you know these Englishmen — they're all terrible liars."

Mike tripped and fell into a deep drain. His companions rushed to his assistance and found him lying motionless at the bottom. Pat got down beside him and giving him a shake, asked: "Are you dead, Mike?"

"No," replied Mike, "but I'm speechless."

Paddy was taking his driving test and to the examiner's amazement he went straight through a red light.

"Why did you do that?" he asked Paddy. "We might have been killed."

"Not to worry," grinned Paddy. "The brother, who's an expert driver, told me to drive through the red — he's been doing it for years and he's never had an accident."

A couple of minutes later Paddy drove straight through another red light.

"Look," screamed the examiner, "you really are trying to kill me."

Then they came to a green light and Paddy slammed on his brakes, nearly sending the examiner through the windscreen.

"What the heck did you do that for?" he roared.

"I always stop when the lights are green," explained Paddy; "after all, the brother might be coming the other way."

"**P**at, here's a dollar I borrowed from you last week."

"Sure, Mike, I'd forgotten all about it."

"Yerra, why didn't you say so?"

Pat and Mick went to Dublin for the weekend, and in a high-spirited moment took a double-decker bus for a joy ride. They crashed into a low bridge and made smithereens of the bus. When they appeared in court, the judge asked them why they had not stolen a single-decker bus, in view of all the low bridges they would meet.

"It's Mick here," said Pat, "he likes to go upstairs for a smoke."

Anew McMaster, the Irish actor-manager, when travelling by train in Ireland with his company was one day stopped at a small country town. Lowering the carriage window he revealed his colourful clothing but, unconcerned, he asked the porter: "What country, friend, is this?" The porter promptly gave Shakespeare's own reply: "This is Illyria, lady."

Pat and Mick shared a room when Pat went to visit some friends. The next morning they were checking up on how each had slept.

"Well, Pat, did you hear the thunder last night?"

"No, Mike. Did it really thunder?"

"Sure it did, as if heaven and earth would come together."

"Why didn't you wake me man? You know I can't sleep when it thunders."

Pat's son became an actor and one evening rushed home to his father in a state of great excitement.

"Guess what, dad," he announced, "I've just been given my first part. I play a man who has been married for twenty-five years."

"Keep it up son," said Pat. "Some day you may get a speaking part."

Mick was seen leaving the theatre at the interval during a new play.

"Excuse me, sir," said the doorman, "isn't the play to your liking?"

"It's not that at all," said Mick, "it's just that the programme says that the second act takes place two weeks later and my mother told me to be home before midnight."

Pat's young nephew Brian was going on his first date so he asked his uncle for advice.

"Should I kiss her unexpectedly," Brian asked him, "or should I build up to it?"

"Look, boy," smiled Pat, "you can't kiss a girl unexpectedly, only sooner than she thought you would."

Paddy and Mick were watching a John Wayne film on television. In one scene John Wayne was riding madly towards a cliff.

"I bet you £10 that he falls over the cliff," said Paddy. "Done," said Mick.

John Wayne rode straight over the cliff.

As Mike handed over his £10, Paddy said, "I feel a bit guilty about this. I've seen the film before."

"So have I," said Mick, "but I didn't think he'd be fool enough to make the same mistake twice."

Oil was discovered off the coast of Connemara, but during operations one of the oil wells caught fire and went out of control. So they sent for Red Adair, the fire fighter, who flew in by private jet and soon blew the fire out.

Afterwards an Irishman said to him, "That was terrific. Tell me, do you see anything of Ginger Rogers at all these days?"

"**C**ome on in, Mike," the genial owner of the estate beckoned to the workman hesitating at the gate.

"That's a fierce dog you've got," said Mike dubiously, pointing to an Airedale barking furiously just within the place.

"Don't you know a barking dog never bites?"

"Sure, I know it," said Mike. "What I'm wonderin' is, does that dog know it?"

Pat and Mick were at a bingo session and one of them kept looking over the other's shoulder and telling him when his numbers were being called.

Mick got annoyed and said, "Look, why don't you fill in your own card?"

"I can't," said Pat, "it's full."

When Pat was asked if he would join a nudist colony, he refused. "If nature intended me to be a nudist, I would have been born without any clothes on," he explained.

The following is a letter to the editor of *The Dublin Times*:

"Dear Sir,

Last week I lost my gold pocket watch, so yesterday I put in an advertisement in your LOST AND FOUND columns. Last night I found the watch in the trousers of my other suit. God Bless your newspaper."

Have you heard about the Irishman who walked into a record store and asked for the latest single by Marcel Marceau?

An old Irish woman was explaining to her neighbour that she didn't like teabags.

"By the time you'd have the corners cut off them and the tea taken out of them you'd have been as well off buying a full half pound of tea in a packet in the first place."

Two Irishmen were boasting to each other how dumb their sons were.

"Let me show you how bad my son Mick is," said the first. "Come here Mick," he said, calling him in. "Here's a pound, now go into town and buy me a Rolls-Royce." Off went Mick to town.

"That's nothing," said the second man. "Wait until you see my son Dinny. Come here Dinny; now go into town to Sullivan's pub and see if I'm there." So off went Dinny.

On the way to town Mick and Dinny met and began to boast about how dumb their fathers were.

"Take my old man," said Mick. "He's just sent me into town with a pound to buy a Rolls-Royce, and every fool knows the salesrooms are closed today."

"That's nothing," said Dinny. "My old man is really the limit. He's just sent me into Sullivan's pub to see if he's there. Couldn't he have just picked up the phone by his elbow and found out for himself in a second?"

First Irishman: "What's Mick's other name?"
Second Irishman: "Mick who?"

And have you heard about the Irishman who used to take two hot water bottles to bed with him?
It was just in case one of them sprang a leak.

Anyone who isn't confused here doesn't really understand what's going on.

Belfast citizen, 1970

" **C**an you tell me what steam is?" asked the examiner.
"Why, sure, sir," replied Patrick confidently. "Steam is — why — er — it's water that's gone crazy with the heat."

" **D**o you dream about me, Pat?" asked Bridget.
"Sure, I can't sleep with dreaming of you darling," answered Pat.

Some Irish inventions:

The one-piece jigsaw puzzle
The inflatable dartboard for campers
An index to the dictionary
Waterproof teabags
A floodlit sundial for night use
A unisex maternity hospital
Boil-in-the-bag cornflakes
A hairdryer which works under water
A solar powered torch

Have you heard about the Irishman who
thought:

Manual labour was a Spanish trade union official?
Slim panatella was a country and western singer?
Chou En-lai was Chinese for bed and breakfast?
Yoko Ono was Japanese for one egg please?

Where would you find an Irishman the day his
boat comes in?
Waiting at the airport.

AN IRISHMAN'S DIGITAL COMPUTER—WITH MEMORY

ALSO AVAILABLE IN LEFT HAND MODEL

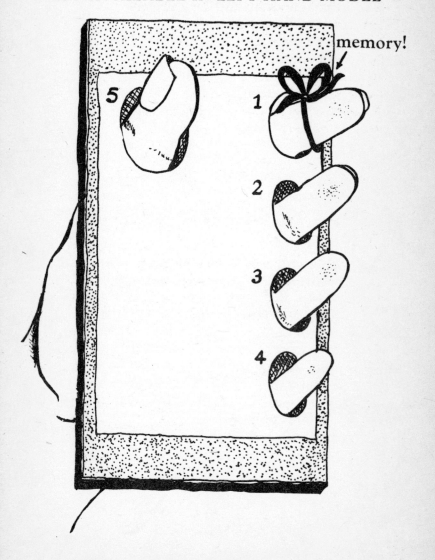

A schools' inspector travelling in Limerick asked a young boy in class, "Who knocked down the walls of Jericho?"

"It wasn't me, sir," said the boy nervously.

Furious with the low standard in the class, the inspector reported the incident to the headmaster of the school.

"I asked a young lad, who knocked down the walls of Jericho, and he told me that it wasn't him."

"The little rascal," said the headmaster, "I bet it was him all the time."

Even more furious, the inspector went to the school manager and repeated the story.

"Well," said the school manager, "the boy comes of an honest family, and you can take it from me, that if he says he didn't knock down the walls of Jericho, then he is telling the truth."

Finally, in despair, the inspector reported the whole affair to the Department of Education. He received the following communication:

"Dear Sir,

With regard to your recent letter concerning the Walls of Jericho, we beg to inform you that this matter does not fall within the jurisdiction of this department. We therefore suggest that you refer the problem to the Board of Works."

An Irishman went to college and got B.A., M.A. and Ph.D. degrees in literature but couldn't get a job, so he went to England to work on the buildings. The foreman decided to give him a test before he would take him on.

"What's the difference between a joist and a girder?" he asked.

"Well," said the Irishman, "Joyce wrote *Ulysses* and Goethe wrote *Faust*."

A fan accosted James Joyce in Zurich with the words, "May I kiss the hand that wrote *Ulysses*?"

Joyce refused, saying:

"No, it did a lot of other things, too."

An Irishman was asked how many honours he had obtained in his Leaving Certificate.

"Three," he replied. "Applied Mathematics and Pure Mathematics."

One Irishman was showing off his knowledge to another, so he asked him if he knew what shape the world was.

"I don't," said the second. "Give me a clue."

"It's the same shape as the buttons on my jacket," said the first.

"Square," said the second.

"That's my Sunday jacket," said the first. "I meant my weekday jacket. Now what shape is the world?"

"Square on Sundays, round on weekdays," said the second Irishman.

It was the Irish chess championships and the two Irish grandmasters were sitting with their heads bent over the board, contemplating their strategies. Radio, television and the newspapers waited with bated breath for the next move. Hours went by and there was no sign of anything happening. Then one of the grandmasters looked up and said, "Oh! Is it my move?"

Finally there was the Irishman who was a contestant on *Mastermind*. He chose as his special subject "Polish Popes of the twentieth century".